The Bike
That Spike Likes

Written by Bill Kirk

Illustrated by Jessica Clerk

This is the bike that Spike likes.

These are the people who made the bike that Spike likes.

This is the big truck that moved the bike that
Spike likes.

These are the people who carried in the bike
that Spike likes.

This is the big store with the bike that
Spike likes.

This is the man who will sell the bike that
Spike likes.

14

These are the people who will buy the bike
that Spike likes.

Who is this boy who rides and rides? That's
Spike with his new bike!